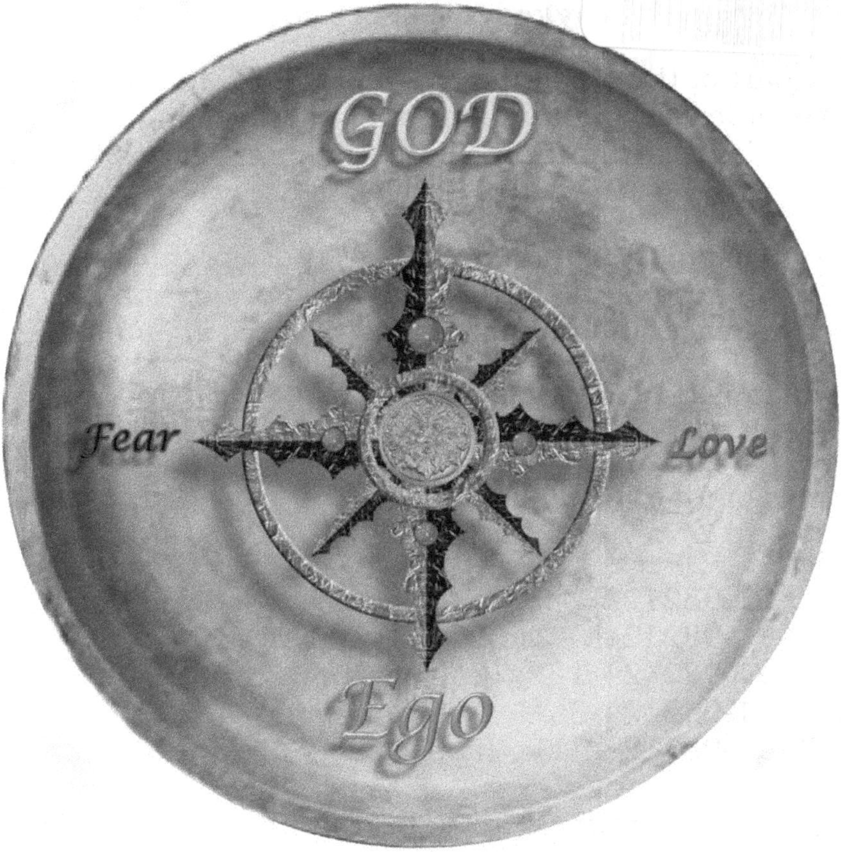

A Course to Miracles

Lars Gimstedt

© **PsykosyntesForum, 2014**

No part of this book may be reproduced in any form, except for the quotation of brief passages in criticism or reviews, without the expressed permission of the publisher: mail@psykosyntesforum.se.

Ideas expressed in this book are those of the author and do not reflect the views of The Foundation of Inner Peace, the publishers of *A Course in Miracles*.

Edition 1, 11 stories.
(Contribute with more stories! See the last chapter.)

Revision date November 11 2014.

ISBN
978-91-982124-2-6   (Kindle version)
978-91-982124-0-2   (EPUB version)
978-91-982124-1-9   (LIT version)
978-91-982124-3-3   (PDF version)
978-91-982124-4-0   (Paper back)

The Kindle version is available on Amazon.com and other Amazon internet stores. The other versions, including the Swedish versions, are available at
http://psykosyntesforum.se/
A_Course_To_Miracles.html

Book cover and illustrations designed by the author. Typefaces Bookman Old 12, Courier New 12 and Segoe Print 11. Page size 6x9" (15,24x22,86 cm) Margins: hor 2,0, vert 1,75.

About the author:

Lars Gimstedt works as a psychotherapist in Linkoping, Sweden. His formal training was as a quantum physicist, and he has worked as an engineer and a manager in corporate business for 30 years.

In the middle of his life, he started to study Psychosynthesis, CBT and NLP, and worked part time as a psychotherapist during ten years, until he started to work full time in his company PsychosynthesisForum.com in 2003 with life and leadership coaching, psychotherapy and with internet e-courses and e-books.

Previous books by Lars Gimstedt:

Stairway. 10 Steps to heaven. (March 2014)
I, Yeshua. Awakener. (May 2014)

Index

Foreword 5
1. Struggling with God. 11
2. Forclosure 16
3. The SMS. 27
4. Coming home to roost. 31
5. To perceive or to See. 34
6. The Awakening. 37
7. Email quarrel. 39
8. A Holy Instant. 44
9. Why are you waiting here? 51
10. Journey to freedom. 54
11. From doubt to peace. 59
12. [Contribute with more chapters!] 63

Foreword

The purpose of this book

This book is a joint venture, where most of the material has been contributed by others. My role has been the one of editor and translator (it is available in Swedish as well). The "others" are fellow students of the book **A Course in Miracles** (ACIM), and I came into contact with them through the web sites MiracleShare.org and the Swedish site Mirakelkursen.org.

The purpose of this book is to bring the message of ACIM "down to Earth" by collecting a number of testimonies of what happens when one surrenders to The Holy Spirit and lets Him decide what to do and what to say.

My hope is that you, reader of this small book, shall overcome any resistance towards surrendering to God you may still have (a common one, I tell you...) and that you will experience God's grace for yourself.

What made me compile this book?

I came across ACIM 1986, or I should rather say, ACIM found me. My wife at that time was a spiritual seeker, whereas I was a square-headed engineer and physicist, atheist by upbringing and scientific training. Relocating for a year to Boeing in Seattle accelerated my wife's interest, as Seattle at the time was somewhat of a Mecca for New Age in the US. One day she brought home a pamphlet about a channeled book, where the alleged author was Jesus Christ. This made "my cup to overflow", as my patience with my wife's "irrational" interests had worn thin during the fall, and I strangely enough decided to read the book (ACIM), with the purpose of convincing my wife of the falsity of material like this one.

To make a long story short[1], this lead to a spiritual awakening for me, in the middle of my life (I turned forty in September 1986). "Doing the course" led to a change of profession, into becoming a psychotherapist and life coach 1992. I have used ACIM as my guide, both in my personal and in my professional life, for almost thirty years now.

Starting to semi-retire from my psychotherapeutic practice at the age of sixty-five made me "return to the origin", that which had made me take the path I once long ago had taken, and I returned to studying ACIM again.

I found that I read the book "with new eyes" (the therapist's), which prompted me to compile an e-course "A Psychosynthesis Perspective on A Course in Miracles", and in short time I also wrote two novels, "Stairway. 10 Steps to Heaven." and "I, Yeshua. Awakener", both based on the message of ACIM.

All this made me reflect deeply on how I was "living" the principles of ACIM myself. To my dismay I discovered that despite my very long practice of working with ACIM as my professional value base, and now even writing courses and books about it, my ego was still in charge of making all my plans and was still the decision-maker (although I suspect Someone Else luckily had nudged me along at times...). ACIM was still quite "theoretical" for me, and I had never really trusted God to decide for me. I had

---

[1] Read my partly self-biographical book "Stairway. 10 Steps to Heaven".

more peace of mind compared to before 1986, but I had not really experienced anything miraculous.

Re-reading ACIM, and for example coming across "The Rules for Decisions" in Chapter 30, finally made me decide *not* to decide myself any longer:

1. *Today I will make no decisions by myself.*

2. *If I make no decisions by myself, this is the day that will be given me.*

3. *I have no question. I forgot what to decide.*

4. *At least I can decide I do not like what I feel now.*

5. *And so I hope I have been wrong.*

6. *I want another way to look at this.*

7. *Perhaps there is another way to look at this. What can I lose by asking?*

Very soon after this decision, I began to experience my first real miracles. Not any mind-boggling or spectacular ones, but I still recognized them as miracles, and I recognized how they corresponded to the descriptions made in Chapter 1, "The Meaning of Miracles", for example these ones (my underlinings):

4. *All miracles mean life, and God is the Giver of life. His Voice will direct you very specifically. <u>You will be told all you need to know</u>.*

11. Prayer is the medium of miracles. *It is a means of communication of the created with the Creator*. Through prayer love is received, and through miracles love is expressed.

18. A miracle is a service. It is the maximal service you can render to another. *It is a way of loving your neighbor as yourself*. You recognize your own and your neighbor's worth simultaneously.

21. Miracles are natural signs of forgiveness. Through miracles *you accept God's forgiveness by extending it to others*.

38. *The Holy Spirit is the mechanism of miracles*. He recognizes both God's creations and your illusions. He separates the true from the false by His ability to perceive totally rather than selectively.

When reading principle 7 *"Miracles are everyone's right, but purification is necessary first"*, I had to confess to myself that my "purification" seemed to have taken almost thirty years...

These experiences deepened my understanding of ACIM by being experiential and emotional rather than just theoretical. I soon felt a need of documenting them in a diary, and I had the idea that this diary could eventually become a book.

After a while I although also felt that the progress with this book-to-become was way too slow, due to the fact that my life nowadays is overall quite tranquil and conflict-free, despite the fact that we, my wife Hildigerdur and I, still have two teen-agers living with us.

Following my new decision in life, I asked The Holy Spirit what to do, and got the answer that I should ask others to contribute, and I published a request for this in the web groups mentioned in the beginning of this foreword.

These contributions follow here below. I have entered them in chronological order, after the date when they were written or the date they were sent to me. I have not commented or written anything about the stories you are about to read, as I think that they speak for themselves.

Enjoy and reflect!

One more thing that I wish to share with you:

On a week-end retreat in October 2014 with the Swedish ACIM network there was a poster greeting us each day as we entered the conference room. The message on the poster was something like this, and it made my spirits lift:

> *Good morning*
>
> *This is God.*
>
> *Today, listen within, and I will give you a solution for any problem you encounter.*
>
> *You need not figure anything out by yourself, so relax and have a good day!*

And finally: please, **contribute** with more personal stories! (Read the instructions in the last chapter.)

A Course to Miracles Lars Gimstedt

1. Struggling with God.

By Pia Rönnquist. Excerpt from the blog
http://ekim.cefeus-kelpie.com/#post234
April 1 2013

After a messy part of my life had followed a long period of relative peacefulness. I continued to read and study ACIM for a couple of years, but after that it became less and less. After all, I had three kids, of whom Patric was still small. A house, a job, and raising dogs.

What I've consciously have worked on during these years is forgiveness. To not let people irritate me, which, to make matters worse, has been near enough impossible since I react so strongly. But I feel so bad when I judge others. As a dog-breeder you are "mommy" to lots of people. As long as they don't ask for help you have to stay quiet, and when they do ask for help, you should have helped them yesterday.

What I did always make sure of was to ask God to help me mate my dogs with the right male, and even to help me sell the right pup to the right owner. Truth be told, the results have been fantastic, I've had fantastic results with the dogs. And I've had wonderful pup-buyers who now, some of them, have bought three and four pups from me.

Although I still participated in competitions a fair amount, this was nowhere near at the same intensity as before. The nature of my work has meant that I've met a lot of different people, and almost every week I'm served another long life history. Whether I've helped anyone, I don't know, but I know I've gained a lot of life experience.

I've also been happy with my family life, and I've been so grateful about Patric that I've almost hoped that there might be something dysfunctional - some learning disability perhaps - about him so that I could keep him with me for the rest of my life. My two older kids both got themselves good educations and moved away.

And at this point my ACIM started to nudge me now and then. I had kept my newsletter subscription with Miracle Center throughout this period, but I hardly read any of them. One of the reasons why I did not want to connect with others was that I didn't want to get involved in the "Who's Closer to God? You or me?" game, and I felt I was leaning in that direction. So I resisted connecting up.

But, then I started having difficulties with my job. In fact, I felt like most things were against me. I broke my leg in the summer of 2009, just as I had gotten going losing weight and started competing again with a new dog. I sat down and felt really sorry for myself, I gained some more weight and I hit 275 pounds in the winter of 2011.

At that point something happened. Enough! I decided stop moaning and do something about it. I started shedding pounds, and began enjoying myself again. Someone had reached down with a screwdriver and adjusted some important settings in my head. It worked with such ease, so I knew help had arrived. And as the pounds kept dropping off me I realized I could not avoid ACIM anymore.

In less than ten months I had shed half my body weight, and with ease. But I also grew scared again. But I thought, OK it is time. I searched the Internet and found ACIM as an audio book. I started listening again, and I listened, and listened. Later that spring I found ACIM in a Swedish translation which meant that now I "had" to start my lessons again. I can't claim that I started of my own free will this time either, instead, it was time for another depression. This one I walked myself out of, some days as far as 30 kilometers - although mostly 14-16 kilometers a day. I was bitten by a dog; I spilled boiling water on my hand, and I fell off my horse and broke one of my fingers and damaged another finger joint.

I was now like a child who wants her reward for starting up with the lessons again, but instead the misery just kept piling on. I realized it was time to give up.

So I began looking for others who also studied ACIM. I joined a Norwegian Facebook group, and I joined the Swedish ACIM group as well. I asked for God's help in finding a better job and then an old colleague of mine called me. He set out on a bunch of small talk but after a while I interrupted him and said, *"You want to offer me a job, right? That's okay. I accept."* Utter silence at the other end of the line, but I was right. And God had helped me again.

At this time the Swedish ACIM translation was published as an audio book and I bought it right away. Now I could listen to it as much as I wanted which was more or less all the time. I found out about more Internet Hangouts, where several ACIM students met, and I joined them, too. I introduced one of my pup-buyers in town to ACIM and she has now begun to read it, and shortly after that I ran into a man who had ACIM on his bookshelf, although he wasn't reading it. Now, we three meet once every two weeks to study the course together. So now I'm in contact with so many. Sure, the old "*Who's Closer to God, You or I?*" has reared its ugly head now and then, but less and less so. And if someone offered some nugget of wisdom that I have been well aware of for at least twenty years, I could feel the impulse to inform him or her of that fact. My ego is still in good shape, doesn't miss a trick...

It's taken me quite a while to let go of my resistance, and it's perhaps not all gone yet even if I feel both confident and calm these days. The lessons have seemed totally different this time around, a lot of resistance in the beginning, but getting easier and easier. After all, it is so incredibly easy, I just need to forgive and let The Holy Spirit guide me. I've even begun to meditate again. Yes, I do my best to absorb the strength of The Holy Spirit. I ask him to guide me all the time, and I keep a close check on my ego who loves making itself known all the time.

For all the resistance I've put up over the years, He has always guided me. At least it seems that way to me when I look at my past. I always have all I need. I receive all the answers I need. And the one thing I know for certain is that even if I put up a big fight resisting God, I will always return. And God always welcomes me back.

I don't quite know why I'm sharing this with you, I don't even know if it interests you. But if there is one thing I've learned - and I learned this lesson many years ago - when The Holy Spirit asks me to do something, I just do it.

In my defenselessness lies my strength.

2. Forclosure

By Calico Hickey
http://calicounedited.com
December 11 2013

This story is about how I created the Greatest Opportunity out of what appeared at the time to be my greatest heart ache.

It started with me purchasing land and building my 'dream Home'. My Irish Grandmother would share stories of living in Ireland above animals. I was beyond intrigued as a child. Fantasies as a child always included animals and living with them in some fashion!

So starting with raw land, I designed my fantasy. I created a Haven. I created the ultimate of 'tree houses'. I lived among the ponderosa pine boughs. I built the loft of my barn out into the most delightful of spaces. 1500 square feet of Love. I wrote affirmations and words of Love on all the supporting beams and trusses. Underneath the tongue and groove pine were the words that would 'support the fantasy'. Or so I thought.

I built my Idol and named her the 'Laughing Palomino'. The more I put into her, the more unconscious my separation from God became. I created my 'heaven', separate from God. Without my conscious thought, there was a belief structure built up around the Laughing Palomino. I worked on self-sufficiency, heating with the wood, cutting wood from the property while allowing the forests to be healthier, my garden provided much of my food, I worked the cattle that eventually became food, recycled, and 'worked my way into a "giant tangle of beLIEfs". A system that would only Serve Me, by my Willingness to Trust God. But in my case, a system of 'thought' and resulting 'effect', that would become dismantled.

None of this was 'conscious' while my idol, Laughing Palomino, remained unchallenged. But on some level, I knew that the path towards God was away from my isolation on the mountain. I deliberately went to the woods, like Thoreau. And I now See, how I needed to 'deliberately' give up the idol, and move elsewhere to better Serve God. I set this up for me to See. I had to give up what I saw at the time, my greatest love.

This "love of form" was what ACIM calls an idol. Idols are anything that we place as greater than God's Love. My Commitment to See as God Sees, became secondary after managing the Laughing Palomino. My idol was greater than God.

If you have a desire to See God 'the idol has to go'... or change... Since I was dealing with a particularly 'stubborn' illusory form, me, my projected lesson called 'forclosure' was the fastest way back to God, 'to see the separation', 'uncover my Light', 'Join in Love'... call it whatever you will.

However, I came into this world of illusion, as a child searching for something... which I ultimately see as my internal subconscious 'Willingness' to See God. The Background that 'drove me forward' in life.

In my life 'story', to Experience God's Love, I would be required to put my idol up as an offering. Somewhere inside I knew that whether I stayed at the Laughing Palomino or I would leave...either way... my greatest commitment was to be Graced with the Peace of God.

I was to be guided through A Course in Miracles, the Literal interpretation of ACIM. The path was divine and The Lesson Complete...

***

The Laughing Palomino was an extraordinary opportunity. I was to design and build my version of my Grandmother Francis' story. In her childhood in Ireland, she had the opportunity to live above animals. I was always intrigued and finally was able to realize my own version of her story. I purchased raw, unimproved land and built my nest. I learned much and it was an extraordinary life. I purchased a barn kit... and then finished off the loft to live in. Dogs, cats, horses, chickens and a whole lot of Happy!!!

Then this projection started to take over my thinking. I was becoming more and more of a slave to my palace instead of Happy. Another student of ACIM asked me once… "*What kept you from Seeing God and Continuing the 'happy' at the Laughing Palomino?*" I have only the knowledge that I threw myself into the illusion and it was mine to deal with. And I Know that whatever shows up in my 'video' is access to a 'whole lot of happiness'… it is just mine to Clear. So my 'video' showed up one day as a note informing me that a big bank had purchased my loan from my originating bank.

I Knew I had something to Clear immediately when my loan was purchased, as my statements changed. The new bank changed my 30 year fixed rate note. My balance went up and my monthly payment went up without any correspondence to me. The new big bank just gave me an 800 number.

This was the beginning of a five year projection that would knock more than my socks off. I spent hours and money on lawyers. The banks had gone postal. I only had an 800 line to sort out 'saving' my home.

The drama continued with the bank posting notes on the gate to the Laughing Palomino. The big bank did not even have a branch in the entire state of New Mexico, but they still had paid employees in my rural area to post 'warnings' and to come to my property to take pictures. The whole situation was delusional from the beginning.

I had many in my life at the time that kept telling me to 'fight them'. "What they are doing is wrong"… So I fought the bank. I fought for a few years before I started to See. All of them were my projections. Another ACIM student asked me once: "*It took 5 years!*"… Yeah, I had a particularly hard head!

A Major Lesson in the world of 'no hierarchy' of miracles... I have never been bound by the 'Laws of God'... which occur as reverse in the 'Laws of the World'. So actually, the thought *"I am right and have the law on my side to prove it"*, actually made me stop myself and remember... I am under by the Laws of God ONLY, which is LOVE. That world has no 'wrong or right' or 'the law is on my side'... so as I allowed the Rule of God, The Love of God to Enter, 'forclosure' started to seem not so 'wrong'. THE MIRACLE: I was starting to SEE this Differently and it meant END OF SUFFERING!

At some point in this I started to speak a commitment for wanting Peace in my Life. I was also guided to See as God Sees. The bank had no such commitment. So finding resolution with different commitments seemed like a folly. So if I was to turn this around once again, I had to See it differently. I started by correcting my speaking about it.

During the early part of this journey, I was referring to the bank as 'stealing my Home'. I saw that by keeping this alive in my speaking, I was creating my perception and in that perception I was further victimizing myself. So as a way to start the process of forgiveness, I had to start somewhere and the place where I started was to correct my speaking, whenever I was lucky enough to hear myself.

I would like to say here, I am a former 'conspiracy theorist and activist'. What I am Learning is that I have seen governments, politicians, and other forms of 'out there' as bad guys to be used as the focus of my anger. The good news at the time was that they were out of range to be hurt through me purporting violence on them. Although, I did have some wild fantasies. The bad news: I was keeping myself victim to the world I saw and subsequently made wrong. My beLIEf was *"This can never be a 'happy' place.... NEVER"*.

So I started praying and sitting in God's lap with all of it. I started to dissemble what happened to me. I lived in a house... then I moved. Without any trauma or drama, this is clearly what happened (without any story). I kept correcting my thinking from *"stealing a house"* to *"leaving a house"*. At some point the spark and anger were gone. I am not sure how this all came about except from <u>a small willingness</u> to See all of this differently and a vigilance of minding my thoughts.

I also had a great deal of assistance from a retreat with Nouk Sanchez. I took all of my ACIM teachings and moved them out of metaphor land. I was frustrated that I would be accepting the atonement for the bank, for the rest of my Life. How could I truly be peaceful within a delusional world. Nouk was the first ACIM teacher I came across that addressed ACIM as *Literal*. But, I was all in. I had no desire to continue to root around in forgiveness for a bank for the rest of my life. I wanted Peace and Happiness. And I wanted it Now.

And little did I know at the time how powerful a thought process I was entering.

***

In my efforts to 'save' my home, I was writing letters and making calls to everybody. The Controller of Currency (where banks get their money), politicians, lawyers, nonprofits for saving homes, clinics for saving homes, everything but being able to talk to the bank... At this point, the bank still had only an 800 number to call. It would be eventually answered by some minimum wage person that was just attempting to earn enough money to pay their own bills.

There was no way to communicate with anybody other than the person that answered the 800 line. Under no circumstances were we (the public) able to speak to 'the Underwriters'. They were the next people up the bank food chain from the folks answering the phones. The Underwriters supposedly had some influence and made probably a couple bucks more an hour than the minimum wage employees answering the phones.

I must say, in all of this - the folks answering these big bank 800 numbers are the real heroes. They spend eight hours a day answering 'angry phone calls'. In my mind, this would be 'hell on earth'. These poor people are being asked to take on something similar to the Jews that were forced to play music while their friends walked to the gas chambers…

Later, I wrote letters of expressing my thankfulness to several of the over fifty people I spoke to over the years at the bank. Some of these individuals did actually attempt to help. I could feel their compassion. I Joined with them in their compassion and separated them from my thoughts of the bank.

My forgiveness was only able to operate within thinking of 'individuals like me'. As soon as it switched to "Them"… "Big Banks", "Evil Empire", "Fukushima", "Monsanto"…whatever, I was off and running into victimizing myself (yet again). So I kept it pretty simple at first, I put people's faces in the place of 'My Angst". I did well many times, did not so well many others. I was in an emotional rodeo with myself.

My apparent choices from my small mind's point of view, included facing (what looked like at the time) the greatest heartbreak I would ever experience or death. Understand that at the time I was not conscious of this, and death through suicide would bring up too much shame. So I 'chose' uterine cancer, a cancer in my womb, my identity's Home.

Banks and cancer had come into my life only as opportunities for me to See God. Students of ACIM have asked me, *"Why did you choose such harsh lessons?"*... Harsh mind, hard head... I don't know. All I do know is that these situations presented themselves to me *by* me. The Divine inside of me summoned exactly what I needed at any given time to get me back to God. Just different forgiveness opportunities having the same solution: Change My mind about Everything.

My small mind received much support from others on how wrong this was. My God Mind though wanted Peace and Love. I could at the time handle become Peaceful with the bank. I was as yet not so sure about the Love part, so I now started off with Making Peace.

And again, being completely honest here, I 'knew' at this point, 'making peace' meant that I had to give up the fight, another true cliff hanger:

A Course to Miracles Lars Gimstedt

***

After having resolved the issue of Wanting Peace more than I wanted a house, I dismantled my family. I found 'great homes' for my animal family, had a huge 'Give Away-party' for the rest of my 'stuff'. I invited my friends, had a big potluck, had 'the kids Marimba band' play (from Santa Fe, a very well-known group called Ande, always referred to as the Kid's Marimba band, even though they are now reaching their 30's). We had the potluck upstairs in my home, while I had put everything I was to not take with me down in the barn. I had set up long tables with all the baubles of a life. I was so aware that where I was going, none of the baubles would be helpful or desired.

The party became an amazing celebration for me. I heard later that those that were there had a great time as well. I did not go downstairs to the 'staging area for the Clearing". I had a couple of friends handle the 'give away'. Everything had to go... so with harness, cart, saddles, stained glass studio, clothes, kitchen and garden equipment, furniture, art, icons, everything was to go to new homes. My desire was to become CLEAR. And I was CLEAR that it included removing many of my toys (former distractions).

A funny side note - and there are many - I was insane about Christmas. Lights, decorations, and do dads. I understand that my Friends handling 'the give-away' were requiring anybody taking something had to also find some Christmas things to take as well. They really were like 'give away nazi's'...forcing Christmas stuff on ALL. I must say I miss none of it, although my tool box was given away as I left it in the barn by accident, it went along with a few more Christmas ornaments. And when I realized that I had no hammer, a friend had an extra and gave me one. Lesson: I need nothing, no thing.

The move from the Laughing Palomino was Magical and so very Easy. I had had an office in town for twenty years and I just moved in there. Actually, friends and patients showed up and moved me in so many ways! And the Peace that came with the decision to 'stop fighting' was like a drink of cool water in desert heat. There were other issues to Clear (cancer and no income), however, the 'structure of thinking' that I laid down during this foreclosure was a 'groundbreaking Foundational Structure of Thinking Through God's Mind'. It has served me very well in all areas of my 'video'.

Closing on the sale was a bit bumpy. I got so angry while signing the 'new official document that is now legally binding', I actually tore the paper writing, '*fuck you bank*' after my 'official signature'... so I am far from perfect. But my forgiveness came quickly as I Cleared! The woman that handled the sale, actually presented me with a cake a while after I tore the official document - a sweet chocolate cake decorated with '*Fuck You [Big Bank]*' (name withheld here to protect the innocent.)

So for now, this Forgiveness opportunity is closed. I experience so much gratitude to My Self for removing the veils that kept me crazy. And I really want to say Thank you to All who have Stood beside me and those that did not. Given my level of insanity, I Bailed on My Self… Then I Chose Again…

So the New Beginning started off in town with two dog companions and a Whole New Way of Looking at Everything! Whooo Hooo, on to New Adventures, With God!

3. The SMS.

By Lars Gimstedt (PsychosynthesisForum.com)
August 10 2014

We have had the tradition of celebrating the days when we got our two adopted children. We got them as infants, and our son Jakob is today 16, our daughter Signý is 14.

During Signý's day this year we were on vacation, out in a sailboat we had rented, so we promised her that we would celebrate her the evening we came home after the week, and that she could have anything she wanted for dinner. At this, she wished to order special pizzas from Pizza Hut.

Shortly after having arrived at our home, we order the pizzas over the telephone and I leave with the car to get them. Driving home surrounded by the scent of the new-baked pizzas makes my mouth water - food aboard the boat had been OK, but you can't really bake pan pizzas in a small galley.

Eager to sit down to eat, I get disappointed with the fact that nobody has prepared anything for the celebration dinner - making the table, fixing soft drinks, and so on.

I point this out to Signý, who met me at the front door, and I say angrily

- "I am going to eat my pizza by myself, before it gets cold!"

Signý also gets angry and retorts

- "You never asked us to do anything!"

I get myself fork and knife, a glass and a can of beer, and seating myself at the dinner table I say

- "You should have understood that by yourself when I drove away to get them."

Signý mimics me and says with a whining voice

- "I am going to eat my pizza by *myself*, before it gets cold!"

Boiling with anger I grab their pizza boxes, lock them into the car, and I rush down into the TV room in our basement with my own pizza and my beer. I wolf the pizza down without any enjoyment, and I then I just remain sitting there, sulking and brooding.

I can't come over my anger despite the fact that my wife comes down and asks me what this all is about. She has fetched their pizzas with her own car key, and asks me to come up and join them. I refuse.

Even when our son comes down and begs me to come up and make peace with his sister, I refuse.

After a while, maybe half an hour, I have calmed down and I start to think about what happened, and about what to do now. I feel deeply ashamed of my childishness. In my thoughts I go through different scenarios for making peace with Signý, but each time I end up in seeing myself being righteous about my own behavior and in making her feel guilty, under the pretense of "making peace".

It feels completely hopeless, until the thought comes

- "I am trying to *analyze* this, and I am trying to be The Holy Spirit myself. Or I am trying to bring *Him* to the problem, instead of bringing the problem *to* Him."

And I pray

- "Please, I ask You, take my anger and my shame. Guide me."

I return up to the kitchen, hoping to find her, but my wife says that she just left to be with a friend living nearby, and that she didn't say when she would come back. So much for the celebration...

I start to make up new scenarios for what to do when she returns, but this time I catch myself immediately, and I pray again

- "Please. Guide me."

And I am led to my desk, and I pick up my mobile, and I send Signý a SMS:

- "*First I demand of you to be able to read my mind. Then by eating by myself, I punish you for not being a mind-reader. Today I really broke my personal record in being dense.*"

Signý promptly replies

- "*Forgive me pa for what I said and did. When shall I be home?*"

I reply

- "*Sometimes we end up in 'trash ping-pong' with ill-considered words. My, my... Come home around ten so you have time to take a shower before going to bed.*"

Signý comes home at ten sharp. None of us say anything, we just walk up to each other and embrace. A long, warm, loving hug...

The other ones in our family don't know anything about our SMS conversation, so later when they are alone with me they both express surprise over the sudden reconciliation. That we didn't trash it out, that Signý didn't stay in her usual teen-age martyrdom.

Feeling complete inner peace, I don't answer, I just smile in response.

4. Coming home to roost.

By Kay Nieminen
September 8 2014

Finding another house to move to was a funereal experience to my mind! I was in mourning and loss as leaving my house - my home, my security and my safety blanket of 21 years was like a death to me. I was leaving an oasis with all its comforts - where everything had its place, where it had everything that I thought I needed, and everything was ordered the way I liked - and I was moving into unfamiliar territory and a future that was unknown and rather scary.

After finding another place to live and before we actually moved, my mind was in chaos. To try and overcome the fear my mind wanted to arrange the furniture and everything that I was taking into the new place, so I could feel some semblance of familiarity and control. I couldn't see how anything would fit or where anything would go. The plain and simple of it was that it wasn't like my home was, and it felt like I would never feel at home again.

With tears rolling down my face and my heart aching with loss I asked the Holy Spirit what was going on and I was told that there is no loss, only transfiguration. I was told that the puzzle pieces no longer go where they used to as my mind (life) was being turned upside down. There was no way that my old furniture would fit nicely into a different landscape and it was symbolic of trying to fit the old into the new. I had no idea what transfiguration meant, so I looked it up and it means: "*a complete change of form or appearance into a more beautiful or spiritual state*". That is certainly not how I saw it then!

A few weeks later I had a revelation and the miracle arrived and this is what I saw:

For many years I yearned to go home and the yearning left me feeling bereft as I didn't know where home was. I had a knowing that it wasn't a yearning for my childhood home and even when buying and owning my own home the feeling and desire to go home was always with me. The confusion of not knowing where this home was only amplified the feeling of emptiness, insanity, loneliness, isolation and depression.

Although owning my own home didn't alleviate the yearning, I had still erroneously placed my sense of safety, peace and belonging to the house. By selling the house and moving, something was dislodged within me and I came to the realization that I had been seeking a home outside of myself to fulfill my needs of emptiness and separation. I had been seeking a sanctuary in the world to give me peace of mind and joy, and when peace and joy seemed to be continuously elusive, the more despairing and fearful life became, the more I withdrew from life and stayed home!

Even though some years back The Holy Spirit had told me that the Home I was seeking was with a capital H - Heaven/God, I still didn't understand that Home was not outside of me so the seeking without continued.

Through the revelations of a miracle brought about by moving house and once again really touching the sense of homelessness, I realized through the process of grieving and tears that what I was yearning for was a place to roost within - a place, a home within myself where I could rest in peace and joy. Tears of grief turned to tears of joy and gratitude as I finally realized that I AM what I had been seeking all this time and all I have to do is to go within and I am already at Home!

Deep gratitude filled my heart as my prayers had been answered and I now can rest in the peace that I AM. A transfiguration has truly occurred as my home had "*a complete change of form or appearance into a more beautiful or spiritual state*" and I moved into my Home.

God is with me. I live and move in Him.
Lesson 222

God is with me. He is my Source of life, the life within, the air I breathe, the food by which I am sustained, the water which renews and cleanses me. He is my home, wherein I live and move; the Spirit which directs my actions, offers me Its Thoughts, and guarantees my safety from all pain. He covers me with kindness and with care, and holds in love the Son He shines upon, who also shines on Him. How still is he who knows the truth of what He speaks today!

Father, we have no words except Your Name upon our lips and in our minds, as we come quietly into Your Presence now, and ask to rest with You in peace a while. AMEN.

5. To perceive or to See.

By Patrick Madden
http://about.me/patrick_madden
September 17 2014

Carl Rogers, among the founders of the humanistic approach (or client-centered approach) to psychology, is believed to have coined the term "unconditional positive regard".

Well, I had a colleague one time for whom I had nothing but "unconditional negative contempt". She and I just did not like each other and did not get along at all. In fact, I was convinced she was doing more harm than good (we are both in the helping profession). I judged her frequently and harshly. She, not surprisingly, reciprocated. We could not function in meetings or on committees together because the sparks would fly and our supervisor, wisely, kept us apart.

I was studying the Course at the time and decided, while learning about "seeing with the vision of Christ", to accept her presence in my life as a learning opportunity. I just could not bear the tension, anxiety, anger, and critical judgment that flew, like sparks, between us anymore. I was even losing sleep over it - literally.

As instructed by the Course [Lesson 78], I began praying for guidance from the Holy Spirit so that I could get to the place where I could let go of my judgments of her and simply forgive her. During my morning meditations I began trying to visualize her in my mind as clearly as I could and, once I had the image I would strive to "see past" her physical appearance (facial features, etc.), as well as all the negative characteristics I associated with her.

It took a while (several sessions), but eventually the miracle happened! I actually SAW her as she truly is beneath the earthly persona she presented (or that I constructed). What I saw was simply (well not simply!) radiant white light emanating from her. It was absolutely glorious! I cried a lot that morning - for joy - for I had succeeded in transforming my hatred for her (a reflection of my own fear and self-loathing) into love for her. I saw her as she truly is, always was, and always will be. At that moment, all judgment and hatred for her melted away. How could I hate that radiant being? Along with the hatred I had for her I my hatred for myself melted away too; for I realized that she was I and I was she, and we are both divine beings.

And the best part of that experience is I realized I could do this with anyone and everyone. I now knew FROM PERSONAL EXPERIENCE that the teachings of the Course are real!

Since that time I have been able to SEE many individuals because, thanks to my former 'enemy', I now know what to look for. It is an amazing and wondrous experience. It has changed my life.

Subsequently, when we would be in the presence of each other I found that I was no longer sending out the negative, electrically charged, judgmental energy that I had been directing her way. I practiced SEEing her in real life as I had seen her during my meditation. Apparently she "got it" that I was no longer willing to be at war with her. And, viola! she stopped sending hostility and judgment and negativity my way. We were at peace.

Although we did not end up working together very much after that (different assignments in our organization), we did attend meetings together and pass in the hallways. The obvious LACK of tension was amazing. We did not become best friends or choose to go out to lunch together. But, we did cease to dislike or attack each other. She even came to my retirement party (not at all like her to attend social functions), and we smiled and hugged each other.

I still bless her for being in my life. She taught me a HUGE lesson. Sometimes, those with whom we have the most difficulty in life are our most important teachers.

Lesson 78: "Let miracles replace all grievances."

May the light of our Father's Loving Heart bless and refresh all who will receive it.

6. The Awakening.

By Hanle, South Africa
September 18 2014

I was doing my morning lesson. In the quiet I was asking once again for peace. Then, I suddenly heard the Holy Spirit saying clearly that it is there, waiting for my acceptance. When I opened my eyes, it was as if I walked into a different world. Everything around me was so beautiful, filled with love. I remember getting into my car, looking down at the steering wheel and I saw that it was Love. As I was driving to work, I looked at the trees and they were shimmering with this incredible Love. The air around me was filled with Love. It was as if I re-entered paradise.

I arrived at work and my colleagues were seemingly having a heated discussion about the Bible. But, all I could see was how absolutely lovely they were, each and every one. I had no desire to contribute. I was just filled with glorious Love and It was everywhere, in everything. That morning I heard about three different people who died that weekend and I saw what a silly concept death was.

I saw that it is true that everyone was there with me. It was if our little bodies and egos were in the far, far distant, as if binoculars have been turned around. Whilst we were pretending to work, to chat, to eat, we were all in a totally different place, which wasn't a place at all. There were no bodies where we were, everything was abstract, yet I somehow knew who I was communicating with. Our communication was total Love, absolute contented Love. Even people I seemed to strongly dislike in the dreamworld, was there with me, in glorious Love and Peace. One of them said to me that he needed to do what he did to help me let go of it all. I saw that every single one was my precious Teacher and that not one was excluded, ACIM student or not, religious or not. We were all totally equal, no one ahead, no one behind.

This was the real world I entered, as opposed to the only sometimes happy dream I experienced before. It was every bit as glorious and wonderful as the Course describes it. It lasted for four wonderful days.

I then had a thought "I must hold on to this" and with that I started returning to the dream. I suffered from severe guilt afterwards. I have been shown what lies beyond the veil and I chose to return and side with the ego.

Later I realized that I could return to the memory of the real world at any moment and it has helped me so much in getting real clear about the teachings of the Course. A sense of deep gratitude replaced the guilt.

I have shared this experience with only a handful of people. It is difficult to find the words to adequately describe it. I have experienced many other miracles, but this was the biggest of them all.

7. Email quarrel.

By Bonnie Nack
September 22 2015

I had an e-mail conversation the other day. It became quite heated and had led nowhere. This is an excerpt from it, from a point just before a miracle suddenly happened:

From: Bonnie Nack <bnack@ca.xx.com>
To: tsumit <tsumit@aol.com>
Sent: Wed, Sep 17, 2014, 9:47 pm
Subject: Re: the whole quote

As usual you use some authority to back up your lies and distortions. I am too tired to even try to cope with them any more. But I am glad you seem to have benefited from our exchange.

From: tsumit <tsumit@aol.com>
To: Bonnie Nack <bnack@ca.xx.com>
Sent: Wed, Sep 17, 2014, 11:46 pm
Subject: Huh?

Hopefully this animosity will blow over at some point. Or, even if it does not, that we can manage to forgive each other internally. I think of myself as a work in progress with a long way to go, but I am not as terrible as you seem to believe. And, as I have said in other emails, I would never have undertaken this difficult process if I did not have high regard for you, and cared about you. It has not been easy for either of us, and I do appreciate your efforts as well as my own. The fun part was the mean genes thing, and yes,

we both have them, but that is OK.
Warmly, Thea

From: Bonnie Nack <bnack@ca.xx.com>
To: tsumit <tsumit@aol.com>
Sent: Wed, Sep 18, 2014, 1:15 am
Subject: Re: Huh?

I do not think you are terrible. I think that most of your thinking is automatic and for that reason meaningless. What I have written to you about your ego defenses was for my own learning, and I hope for yours. I was pleased with myself that I could survive them instead of getting entangled in them. Actually my deepest motivation was to try to establish some rapport with you based upon what was true instead of superficialities.

I had a miracle experience last night. The higher mind or God came and wiped away the meaning from our interactions. The whole thing is meaningless. It was if it did not happen in emotional terms. It is emotions that give events meaning. Meaninglessness is a peculiar experience and I had to consent to letting it happen. A whole segment of my life meaningless? I consented even though it was a little scary.

It appears that the pain in my lower back is healing. The Course teaches that it is not the physical healing that is important; it is the cleansing of the mind that is important. Physical healing follows naturally.

I teach my students something called the Holy Instant. The Holy Instant is the moment when the mind is quiet enough to hear an answer not entailed in the question. I have practiced the Holy Instant for some time, and received much spiritual guidance.

This experience last night was like an expansion of the Holy Instant. I was willing to give up my attachment to our interactions, and their meaning disappeared. The Course teaches that a cause is only a cause when it has effects. No effects, no cause.... no guilt.... nothing happened. That is the miracle that heals.

So I have learned even more from our interaction. I have learned how God or Holy Spirit does miracles. I am more relaxed that before. I know that all I have to do to do miracles is do what I do. Nothing more. Nothing special. Just put one foot in front of the other knowing from the point of view of spirit, nothing matters.

Nothing matters means the world is not real, nor are our suffering real. It is all an illusion. Our interaction seems at this time to have been an illusion or a dream.

I dreamed this morning I had nothing to wear... a huge pile of clothes and nothing to wear. I could not attend school because I had nothing to wear. Animals were climbing onto the pile of clothes... dogs sleeping on them. All were gentle and peaceful.... deeply so. Maura was off on the side concerned about me, not understanding.

No worries, no problems, no pressure... just doing what I have to do moment by moment. Clothes have to do with creating appearances. School has to do with the intellect.

All that in terms of the miracle is meaningless. This world is meaningless. It is our attachment to it that gives it meaning.

From: tsumit <tsumit@aol.com>
To: Bonnie Nack <bnack@ca.xx.com>
Sent: Wed, Sep 18, 2014, 9:39 am
Subject: Re: Huh?

You had some very positive experiences last night. This feels great. I think that all healing is mental. Have heard that more than once.

From: Bonnie Nack <bnack@ca.xx.com>
To: tsumit <tsumit@aol.com>
Sent: Wed, Sep 18, 2014, 10:52 am
Subject: Re: Huh?

You have catalized a great deal of spiritual growth for me. Just now I am realizing that the thing we cherish most in this world... our "I", is the thing we are here to overcome. It is the cause of all suffering.

Both ACIM and Kabbalah teach we are One. The "I" is what separates us. The "I" is made of memories, a self-created image called ego, and ego defenses. Behind that is the universal mind, or One. So the memories, self-image and ego defenses keep us from knowing we are One.

I call the Holy Spirit in The Holy Instant "the great eraser." I did not know how great He is. He can erase your whole personal history if you invite Him to do so.

For myself, it seems such a great relief to be getting rid of the "I." There was a saint called Nitchananda who used to refer to himself as "this one."

ACIM says that the secret agreement we all have between us is to be hurt and attack in return. That is the agreement that keeps us in the illusion we are separate. That is the agreement that supports the ego and self-image. If you cannot be hurt, you have no ego and self-image. Or vice versa, if you have no self-image and ego, you cannot be hurt.

I can feel my body relaxing and healing.... even the joints are releasing. No I, or ego; no need to attack; no need to hurt.

The body is an extension of the mind and only obeys the mind. It has no mind of its own. It is dust.

8. A Holy Instant.

By Daniel Vandinja
Editor of Mirakelnytt (Swedish for Miracle News)
at the Swedish ACIM network, mirakelkursen.org.
September 26 2014
(Translated to English by Lars Gimstedt.)

In my studies of A Course in Miracles, that I have been pursuing for a couple of years, it has been easy for me to accept the metaphysical parts, i.e. the information clarifying how the Universe was the result of separation, projection, guilt, and so on. It has also been relatively easy for me to use the tools for forgiveness offered by the Course, at least the Workbook lessons up to Repetition nr 1.

The lessons after the first repetition in the Workbook have though been more difficult to digest. After Lesson 61 the lessons start to have a different character, from being about how my view of the world can be changed, to how I can change how I see "myself". The lessons are more and more about me and my true nature, and they come with clean-cut statements I am expected to just swallow: *"I am the light of the world"* (61), *"I am as God created me"* (94 plus more similar ones). I have had difficulties understanding and integrating these statements. They have felt too alien, unrealistic and bombastic to be about "me".

But, a Saturday morning in July, this year (2013), A Holy Instant occurred. I awoke in the morning in a state of heavy depression. I thought to myself that there must be a passage in the Course that can help me to counter this feeling of "meaninglessness" so well-known to me, a feeling that has come to me now and then over the last couple of years. I flipped the pages back and forth at random and chapter 31 came up, section VIII.1.5, and the first thing that caught my eyes was the statement

*"I am as God created me. His Son can suffer nothing. And I **am** His Son."*

I read this statement feeling somewhat sceptic, but I still decided to give it a chance. I read it aloud to myself, and gave my recital all the conviction I could muster. After a minute or so the words suddenly came alive to me. A deep, vibrating and shining insight emerged - "These words are TRUE!"
All of a sudden I understood that this statement was really about *me*!

A laughter that completely relieved my tension bubbled up from deep within. A laughter that felt like it ripped my chest open, and that made my eyes burst with tears. I laughed so hard that my neighbors must have thought that I had gone insane. My heart pounded, filled to the rim with humbleness, passion, love, and above all, joy! A joy that even my mind took part in, as a flash of insight of the absurdity of this world. I laughed at how I had ever been able to believe that I am a small body that can suffer and die. This thought now seemed so absurd that I laughed out loud for a full half hour.

There was also, in this instant, a deep feeling of awe and gratitude. I walked, laughing and crying, to and fro between the different mirrors in my apartment.
I bowed to the holy creature, whose living heart filled with love and tear-filled eyes looked back at me, in my bathroom, in my kitchen and in the mirrors in my living-room.

When this "miracle shower" had abated some, after forty minutes or so, I still felt some elation, but this lively feeling more and more gave place to an experience of imperturbable stillness and peace.
I returned to the page I had looked at before in the Course and read the following passage:

VIII. Choose Once Again

1. Temptation has one lesson it would teach, in all its forms, wherever it occurs. It would persuade the holy Son of God he is a body, born in what must die, unable

to escape its frailty, and bound by what it orders him to feel. It sets the limits on what he can do; its power is the only strength he has; his grasp cannot exceed its tiny reach. Would you be this, if Christ appeared to you in all His glory, asking you but this:

Choose once again if you would take your place among the saviors of the world, or would remain in hell, and hold your brothers there.

For He has come, and He is asking this.

2. How do you make the choice? How easily is this explained! You always choose between your weakness and the strength of Christ in you. And what you choose is what you think is real. Simply by never using weakness to direct your actions, you have given it no power. And the light of Christ in you is given charge of everything you do. For you have brought your weakness unto Him, and He has given you His strength instead.

I now understood what I had done - I had "**chosen again**"! A burst of laughter came again, and continued for a good while. "The only thing I need to do is to **choose**!" My thoughts went to the well-known lecturer Kay Pollaks slides with angry and with happy smileys, slides he uses as illustrations in his lectures about choosing joy. This is really the truth, everything is about making a choice. There is although also a good deal of seriousness in this choice that according to the citation above is between whether to *"take your place among the saviors of the world, or remain in hell, and hold your brothers there"*.

This revolutionary insight about the simplicity of this choice, but also about its great importance, made me now hear a voice within myself. I experienced the presence of an elder and wiser brother, just behind my back, to my left. A being full of warmth and compassion.

A thought came up whether to call somebody up on the telephone in order to share my "Holy Instant". Many different persons spontaneously appeared to my inner vision. I picked up the receiver, ready to call the first one of these persons. But at that moment the Voice said, mildly but coercively:

"Think twice about what you are intending to do. How will this person react on what you want to share? Do you know how this person's life is just now? Are you sure this person will be able to appreciate and accept what you want to share? Sometimes an uplifting experience like this can give an opposite result in a person struggling with his or her own life. So your joyous story may then be experienced as an attempt to show yourself off, demonstrating how far you have come in your spiritual development".

I chose to refrain from calling someone, but I wrote an entry in the ACIM network's Facebook page, as I still felt strongly that I wanted to share this joyous experience with others. I got a huge number of wonderful comments that day from other ACIM students.

After this I glanced through the Workbook. Whichever lesson my eyes landed on, each one of them felt completely obvious. It felt like reading a picture book for three-year-olds. Everything felt crystal clear. Everything in the Course is TRUE, everything is in there, completely without any paraphrasings. Everything in the Course is completely straight-forward! It felt like I owned a huge and priceless treasure chest, a chest the worth of which I had not had the wits to understand. Which unbelievable gift this was, to be able to continue to read the Course, and to be able to, with will-power and commitment, put all its statements into living practice.

The creature guiding me from behind felt very familiar to me. It felt like I had met "him" many time before, even at times when it had not been clear to me. It felt like an older, wiser, part of myself, some kind of "higher I" having the ability to see the realm of the Spirit as well as the world of illusions. A Voice whose goal really just is to help us to make wiser decisions. A "Being" whose function is not to take our authority and free will from us, but who rather aims to help us to become aware of which our choices are, and the consequences of these choices. In most cases we know what is "right", but when we go against our intuition, we steer off the road and end up in the ditch, and further out into the bushes. There is a simple road to follow and the Course tells us how to choose in order to travel through our lives with as little pain as possible.

Now, a couple of days after my Holy Instant, I experience my life as easier. I have nothing to "blame" any longer. If I feel depressed, it is only because I am choosing "my weakness" before "The Strength of Christ". Then, the only thing I have to do, is "choosing again". Furthermore, I experience my thoughts as having less impact on my state of mind, they fail to capture my full awareness. They pass me like water poured on a goose. It feels like a glass pane has been set up between me and my thoughts, as if they are fishes in an aquarium with myself standing outside as a spectator. More and more often my thoughts just disappear completely. They do not swim at all. They just vanish like smoke and leave my mind empty, still and at peace. A wonderful state of mind, where the world feels more alive and colorful.

One thought although came up the other day. I was walking up a hill from having been down bathing from the piers home at Kristineberg, in the southern part of Stockholm. I thought to myself: "Now, what is it I want to do with my life?" When I raised my eyes from the narrow foot-path to see where I was heading, I happened to look at an apartment house, and saw that someone had painted the word "DEUS" with a spray can on one of the high walls. (Deus is Latin for God.) I smiled to myself, and thanked The Holy Spirit for His guidance.

9. Why are you waiting here?

By Dr Michael Gottschalk, 62 years old.
January 29 2014
(Translated into English by Gabriela Jaeger)

My JOY that healing happens here in our world -
I would like to share it with you:

For almost two years I have done volunteer work in a hospice for the terminally ill called "Emmaus House" in Wetzlar, Hesse, Germany, in the afternoons and early evenings. I participate in what is called "Room Service". My task is to prepare supper, participate in excursions, running errands and have conversations the guests in my charge.

A few weeks ago a woman came in her mid forty's linear dreamtime to the hospice, and she was placed in the area where I worked.

On her first day at the hospice I was "accidentally" the first of us employees she met and she soon led our conversation into Buddhism and incarnation, near death experiences, about leaving the body and about medical treatment ideas.

She told me her story and, as always in the hospice when inmates share their medical histories with me, I can listen with an open heart by forgiving them for being trapped in their beliefs and thereby releasing their anxiety (in her specific "case", a probably "untreatable" cancer). By this it seems that they have become able to experience peace, comfort, blessing and emotional healing.

After dinner she asked me about my motives for doing hospice work as a volunteer. In the conversation that followed from her inquiry, I could tell her about how totally happy and full of joy I felt as a Course student, especially as she asked what spiritual literature I would read usually.

When I after a while brought her back to her room, I experienced suddenly how we had an eye contact in what felt like an eternal moment, but which afterwards felt like what the Course calls the Holy Instant.

After this she approached me each day, and in our gentle conversations as well as when we just sat quietly together, I could step back and I invited healing to happen in her mind, as well as in mine.

After some time, I was one day directly guided to ask her:

- "What do you actually want here in the hospice? You must surely have better things to do than to wait here for leaving your body?"

In the period after this, I often thought about her, feeling how we were connected in spirit and in blessings, but we did not meet, as I during this period worked there only a couple of days per week.

But, just one week ago she came and sat down beside me and told me that she had been out in Wetzlar during the day to buy new clothes. This is for "guests" of the hospice (as the patients called there officially) extremely unusual.

I told her that I thought this was great - now she indeed could go home again. She said that she had asked for new medical reports, as she wanted to leave next Wednesday, which was yesterday.

When the medical report came, her cancer diagnosis was reported as "negative", i.e. there was no trace of it any longer.

In a book at our reception, where the guests can make entries, I saw after she had left for her home, that she had written "It is quite incredible, but here I experienced such a wonderful care, and it made me feel how I got better each day that passed..."

Healing happens.

Together.

In spirit.

Via the body as a beneficial learning tool.

This happy student of the Course, Michael, has experienced healing at the level of his learning of the Course and with it a quiet miracle, seen as a visible result in the world.

This happy dream I hereby like to share with you.

And I feel that I share this experience in spirit with the affectionate managerial and nursing staff of the hospice "Emmaus House", as someone had entered the words after her farewell entry: "Hooray and thank you!"

10. Journey to freedom.

By Sandy Sparkle, Hungary
October 21, 2014

It was 2012, and I was writing a list of my 100 dreams and desires as an introductory task of a multilevel marketing company. I yearned for freedom. I was fed up with working as an employee only for money in a job I hated and I was bored at. I was fed up with waking up every morning to a thought in my mind: "Oh, no, it's morning again, I don't want to get up and go to work". I was fed up with compromising with my dreams and inspiration. I desperately yearned for freedom.

I thought I have found the solution. I had at this time still the tendency to think that I was the one who knew best what was good for me. I always planned everything in great detail, and I tried to control the outcome. This time it was just the same. I set the goal to be financially independent to be able to do what I wanted and when I wanted. I was convinced that I needed to make more money to have more choices and more freedom. I was determined to achieve financial freedom - which I now see - is a contradiction in terms.

I started to work in the MLM (Multi-Level Marketing) industry so I could be finally free. But all the time, I felt that something was off. I pushed myself further and further with meagre results. I was using people. I was speaking words I did not even believe. I tried to sell products that I did not think were worth their price. I was deceiving myself and I sank deeper and deeper into guilt. All the time, I had a feeling that I was not enough and I should do more. There was like a broken record playing in my mind, saying that I should do a lot more for my future to reach the freedom I was looking for.

2013 was the year when my heart's prayer was Answered. A Course in Miracles arrived in my life. I was so enthusiastic and I felt such trust and an inner knowing that this is it. I knew within that these lessons would change my life. After two weeks of practice I was guided to quit the MLM company. A huge amount of guilt was lifted from my mind. The inward journey began.

Day by day my awareness grew that financial independence was not my true desire. I realized that I had always yearned for the Peace of God, which for me seemed like true freedom. God-dependence as true freedom... Following my Guidance now led me into deep joy and also into collaborations with mighty companions.

2014 I was guided to contact the Living Miracles Community. With this step I gained momentum, and the healing in my mind got really intensive. I invited David Hoffmeister to Hungary, started to translate his books into Hungarian, subtitle his YouTube videos, organize the Hungarian gatherings and retreats. I was guided to quit my daytime job and to immerse fully in the mind training.

But, with this step a tremendous fear surfaced. Despite the savings I had, but without the regular income, an intense and irrational fear dominated my mind. Thoughts of the unknown future kept popping up. I though understood that the ego's dark insecurity had to be exposed to the Light of forgiveness.

Practicing the lessons relieved my mind every day from the idea that freedom is in the future, that it is always something I don't have right now. My goal became now never to waiver from the message of lesson 50:

"I am sustained by the Love of God."

The learning I have reached through this single lesson has been a Divine Gift every moment I choose to remember it. And the result of this learning - miracles - have continually been showing me the way:

When I started to organize the Hungarian events, a donation came in that covered the accommodation of our guests. A Course student contacted me and told me that there was a significant amount of fringe benefit from her previous employer that she wanted to donate because the deadline to use the benefit was the end of that month, and she could only use it for accommodation. The process was namely that in case someone did not use it, the money would go back to the employer, so she had been guided to donate the money to me.

Another miracle was when I unexpectedly was given a scholarship so I could attend a six-day retreat in Dublin, and meet David Hoffmeister and the Messengers of Peace for the first time.

I also realized that miracles occur in unconventional ways as well, in unexpected forms. A lot of times I was not given money, but rather an opportunity to ask for help and collaboration.

An example of this was when I felt guided to video record the gatherings and the retreats. My first thought was to hire someone for money. This was the way I had used to handle things, as it had always been really hard for me to ask for help from anyone because I felt that I owe that person, and I wanted to do everything on my own and be independent. The tour coordinator although suggested that I should be open to new solutions. So I just mentioned to my boyfriend that it would be so great to have someone who could lend me his camera and tripod. Suddenly he said that I should call a guy and ask him. I was really surprised but I followed the inspiration. I received a positive answer. I couldn't believe that it can be so simple and easy.

I feel so happy and so grateful for the convincing job that the Holy Spirit has been doing for me these past months, and it seems to just continue, maybe so my mind can be relieved from my old belief in the world's demands on reciprocity.

With the theme money the Holy Spirit continues to provide me endless opportunities to deepen my trust and to enhance my mind training. Following my Inspiration, hand in hand with the Holy Spirit, I feel how loved and supported I am, in every step I take.

The realization that freedom is not far away in the future shifted my perception entirely, and allowed me to rest joyously in peace in the present moment. When fear knocks on the door of my mind, I can choose again. Every moment.

Living in Divine Providence is The True Freedom we all desire in our hearts. We are free – Now and Forever.

11. From doubt to peace.

By Elsa Laurell, Sweden
November 10, 2014.

In the mid 90's, I one day stayed in bed in a painful migraine attack. This was not the first time this had happened, but this time I had been prescribed some new medicines from the pain clinic, and I was now in such pain that I took them all. But the combination of these new pills did not work well at all with me - I soon experienced a terrible anxiety panic, together with the fact that the pains in my head remained unchanged.

This was such a terrible experience, that I thought I would go out of my mind, it felt like I had to flee from myself not to just die. I prayed to God and to Jesus for relief, but my inner state of pain and panic just increased more and more. The pains made me so dizzy and confused that I did not even think of trying to call for help, I just stayed in bed, paralyzed.

But, suddenly, everything around me turned white with light and the pain subsided. A wonderful feeling of well-being permeated my whole body. I felt so relieved and so happy to be free from both the pain and from the panic attack. At this instant I heard a voice, and it said "**You shall be with me!**"

I did not understand from where these words came and neither did I understand what they meant. It almost sounded as an order, but at the same time not harsh or commanding. But at this moment I did not bother that much about the exact wording, as the most important thing for me was that I had become free from the terrible suffering. I rose from my bed and for the rest of the day I functioned normally, to my utter relief.

After this day, I thought again and again about the meaning of these words, *"You shall be with me"*, and what the source could be. A couple of weeks after it had happened I got the opportunity to share my experience in a church gathering with representatives from the different churches in the town I was living in at the time. Immediately after I had concluded my story, a pastor from the Swedish Missionary Society exclaimed that this must have been Jesus. But, the other priests chose to keep silent... As I had not actually seen a person, just bright white light, I could not claim neither disclaim the presence of Jesus in connection to my experience.

During a long period of time after this extraordinary experience I remained completely free from migraine attacks, but after a couple of months they regretfully returned again.

Now and then thoughts came whether I could have mis-heard and missed one word - "one" - and that the wording really had been "You shall be *one* with me". I also thought a lot about the word "shall". It sounded so commanding, which made me become more and more doubtful whether it really had been a loving spirit that had spoken to me.

I was now and then overcome by these doubts, but at the same time I could never deny my memory of the wonderful feeling I had experienced when hearing the words. To have been blessed to experience such a glorious inner state after having been in such terrible pain, this I could not dismiss from my thoughts and

A Course to Miracles Lars Gimstedt

my memories. Deep down, I was furthermore so grateful for having been allowed to get this glimpse of Heaven, so the exact wording did not really feel that important.

During the years that followed after this, I read a number of books about I-AM-presence with both oneself and with the divine, and I found many things that in different ways confirmed my experience.

Many years ago I was taught a prayer by an acquaintance:
"Holy Spirit, come into me, enlighten my soul and awaken my mind, so I can stay in you".
I have since always used this prayer in moments of pain and difficulties, and each time it has made me feel good again, although not as powerfully as when I heard the words *"You shall be with me"*.

Another thing that struck me was that I many times had experienced a special feeling of greatness and holiness when I had sung the song

"Oh, Great Spirit, earth, sun, sky and sea. You are inside and all around me".

But it was not until just recently, during the summer this year 2014, that I finally realized that it very well could have been The Holy Spirit that had spoken to me. It was when I read "Disappearance of the Universe" by Gary Renard, and it felt like all the bits of a puzzle started to fall into place.

During this fall I then read the second book by the same author, "Your Immortal Reality", where he says a bit into the book:
"The Holy Spirit will not come forth only as a Voice. The Holy Spirit can become revealed in the form of an

intuition, an idea, a feeling or He can speak to you through a person".

"The Holy Spirit can speak to you through your dreams".

And, after having read his third book, "Love Has Forgotten No One", I finally became fully convinced that my experience had really been about The Holy Spirit, especially when I read, a little less than a hundred pages into the book:

"Visualize being surrounded by The Holy Spirit's beautiful, pure, white light".

After this, my old doubt that I had harbored for so many years melted away completely, and it now feels like I have been blessed with a close Friend, both through the experience of His Voice I heard so clearly almost twenty years ago and through my now so strong faith in Who it was that Spoke to me.

Now I feel a constant inner sense of security, a deeper inner peace than ever. I experience a faith that I lacked before. Now I can without hesitation openly say:

*"I **want** to be with You, Dear Holy Spirit!"*

12. [Contribute with more chapters!]

This book is a joint venture, where A Course in Miracle "students" have been invited to contribute short stories about everyday miracles resulting from surrendering one's decisions to The Holy Spirit.

I will continue to ask for new contributions on my homepage (psykosyntesforum.se/A_Course_To_Miracles.html) and on different social media on the internet. My goal is to reach 100 stories!

New editions will be published when new material has been included.

I you have bought the e-book via my web site (see link above), you will be able to download the new edition <u>for free</u> via the download page you received when you purchased the book.

If you sign up for the newsletter connected to the e-course A Psychosynthesis Perspective on ACIM, you will get notified of when new editions are published: psykosyntesforum.se/courses_ACIM.htm .

Go to the web page
psykosyntesforum.se/A_Course_To_Miracles.html
for instructions on how to contribute!

With love
Lars Gimstedt

www.ingramcontent.com/pod-product-compliance
Lightning Source LLC
Chambersburg PA
CBHW060430050426
42449CB00009B/2222